THE GREENHORN'S GUIDE TO CHAINSAWS AND FIREWOOD CUTTING

By Steven Gregersen

Dedicated to our Grandson,
Scott.

Notice

There is always a level of risk involved when using chainsaws and other tools related to harvesting timber.

The information contained here is based upon the author's experience and research and is presented for academic study only. The author assumes no responsibility for it's use or misuse.

The Greenhorn's Guide to Chainsaws and Firewood Cutting

Introduction

I am not a professional logger nor do I cut wood for a living. That doesn't mean I don't know what I'm talking about though. I've been cutting wood for about forty-five-years now and in that time I've learned a few things. Some of that knowledge came through others. My grandfather was my first teacher when I barely had the strength to lift the saw. After that my father-in-law showed me a few new things and in between and afterward I spent time reading books and articles. The toughest education came in the school of hard knocks. That last teacher was the one who got my attention the most effectively and it's the one I'd like to see you avoid as much as possible which is my purpose in writing this book.

I hope you enjoy the book as much as I enjoy my time in the woods cutting our winter's supply firewood.

Steven Gregersen

Chapter One: Choosing a Chain Saw

The first chain saw I ever owned was an old, very used, Craftsman with an eighteen inch bar. It was given to me by my grandfather. It had a cast iron motor and weighed at least twenty-five pounds. It had no chain brake, no vibration dampeners, no muffler or spark arrestor, a "hard nose" bar, and a manually operated pump to oil the chain. It did a great job cutting firewood but it was heavy and dangerous.

Chain saws have come a long way in the last forty years. Modern saws are lighter, safer and easier to use than those in the past. There are more choices and options than ever before and while that's good it can also get a little confusing. So, how do you choose the best chain saw for you? You look over the options then pick the saw that will best serve your needs.

The saw on the left is a McCullough Mini-Mac with a 14 inch bar.
The Saw on the right is a Stihl 029 Super with a 24 inch bar.

Bigger is Better ... Right?

There's a lot of snobbery in saw shops. I remember a year ago when I was visiting my mother in Kansas (about 1500 miles from where I live). She had a couple of dead trees in her yard and remarked that it would cost about a thousand dollars to have them taken out. I told her that if we could come up with a big enough saw I could take care of it. Renting proved impractical, (no one had a saw available at the time), so we purchased a Poulan Pro with a 20 inch bar. It's a decent homeowner's saw but it is a bit underpowered by professional standards.

Anyway, I hit a rock inside the first tree I cut down (must have been some kids who dropped it into a hole in the tree sometime in the past) and nearly ruined the chain. I went to the local saw shop and bought a new chain. He had one that would fit but I was looking for a skip chain. My request surprised him and he replied that they'd have to order it (I guess they don't sell many of those!). Then he snidely commented that a skip chain "was about the only way to get by with a 20 inch bar on an underpowered saw like mine."

My first reaction was to tell him that my big saw was at home but then I held my tongue. I didn't want to get drawn into a "whose is bigger" debate with a sales clerk so I just told him that the "little" Poulan would get the job done. It'd just take a bit longer!

"Size" when speaking chainsaw-ese, refers to power and bar length. Many people, guys in particular, let testosterone override common sense when purchasing a saw and get the biggest motor, the longest bar and the most aggressive chain that they can find. That's not necessarily the best way to do things!

The saw I use most is a Stihl with a twenty-four inch bar. The extra power and bar length enable it to handle larger trees and limbs with ease. It cuts four times as fast as my reserve saw, an 18 inch Homelite. Plus, I don't have to do as much bending over to cut limbs off of trees I've dropped.

But big saws have their disadvantages. The handles are usually larger and spaced farther apart. The longer bar adds extra weight to the front and makes the saw harder to control when cutting. Professional quality saws normally use more aggressive chains that cut faster but which also make them more susceptible to kick-back. In addition, they're expensive.

If you aren't a professional logger, smaller saws have some good points you should consider. First, they cost less than professional saws and second, they're much lighter than full size models designed for either professional or home use. The smaller motors make the saw less intimidating than the fire-breathing, banshee screaming, high-torque saws professionals use. That being said they are slower than a professional saw (especially if you're cutting trees whose diameter is the same as or longer than the length of the bar). If you try to force the chain through you'll just bog down a small saw whereas the professional models just keep chewing through the wood.

Another thing most of us men fail to consider is what will happen if we are injured and can't cut wood. Will our wife or older children be able to cut it while we recover? This is a serious matter if you heat only with wood and can't afford to buy it from a vendor.

My wife's saw is a Homelite mini-saw with a sixteen inch bar. She loves it. Its light, fits her well and she can control it. I used a McCullough Mini-Mac with a fourteen inch bar for over ten years. I've cut over one-hundred cords of wood with it and its still working great. Small saws are quite capable of cutting a year's supply of firewood. They just take longer.

What size saw should you get? You should get the saw you can safely control and afford. Don't buy a big saw just to stroke your ego. Proper fit is far more important than power and bar length.

Reliability

As long as you stay with a major brand reliability is not usually a problem. I've owned saws made by Poulan, Homelite, McCullough, and Stihl, and I've used saws from quite a few other manufacturers. While it's true that you get what you pay for, even low priced saws tend to last a long time with careful use and maintenance. Professional saws are built with better materials and engineering but the difference is not usually going to be a factor for the homeowner cutting his own firewood.

Regular maintenance goes a long way to keep your saw fit for duty.

Fit

A chainsaw should fit you. What I mean by fit is that it should be comfortable to hold and work with. Try different saws and you'll see what I mean. Heft a lot of different saws just to become familiar with the differences in fit. Handle sizes and the spacing between the rear and front handles may vary significantly. Lean over in a position similar to how you'll be when cutting wood. Does the saw balance well or is too much of the weight forward? How does the saw feel with the bar in both vertical and horizontal positions? How about with it held high as when cutting overhead limbs? Is your forward hand too far forward or too far back? Can you reach the trigger easily?

Put on some leather work gloves. Do your fingers wrap around the handles completely? Can you use the throttle trigger while maintaining a good grip? Can you shut it off without taking your hand off the handle?

Is the saw too heavy or the balance point so far forward that when you begin your cut you drop the saw on the limb because you don't have the strength to hold it up? When the saw slices all the way through the limb can you keep the tip from falling to the ground? Is the chain too aggressive or the saw so powerful that you're afraid of it?

This is one of those places where size matters. Long bars change the balance of a saw and make them more difficult to control which can potentially increase the risk of kick-back. A saw that's too heavy in the store will seem to weigh a ton after you've been using it a few hours. Fatigue clouds judgment, makes a person careless, and slows reaction time. Most of the accidents I've had were when I was tired at the end of a long day of cutting.

Should you start with smaller saw until you gain more experience? You're going to be using this thing for hours. Heft a lot of different saws so that you can tell the difference between a good and bad fit.

13

Safety Features

While any chainsaw is inherently dangerous, modern saws are much safer than they were forty years ago. The first saw I ever used had no chain brake, no handle vibration dampers (not even rubber cushions on the handles!) and a chain and bar design that screamed out the words "kickback." Thank God those days are long gone.

In a kickback situation your hand will strike the brake apply handle (which moves forward), tripping a spring operated cam that applies the brake band (the thin metal ring shown in the photo above), squeezing it tightly around the brake drum (the outer housing of the centrifugal clutch). This stops the chain instantly.

Chain Brake

Saws with chain brakes have a bar in front of the forward handle so that if kick-back occurs your hand will strike the bar (which

14

will move forward), applying a brake that instantly stops the chain from spinning. It's the greatest improvement ever made to a chain saw.

Kick-back happens when the upper front part of the chain comes in contact with the wood you are cutting. Because the chain is moving in a circular direction as it revolves around the end of the bar it acts like a spinning wheel (with sharp claws) to launch the front of the bar upward and back if it makes contact with the wood you are cutting.

This might happen if you are (a) cutting up through a limb and the tip of the bar contacts the wood as you begin your cut or (b) if you are cutting down through a limb that's supported on both ends and the limb bends and pinches the upper front part of the chain in the kerf, (c) you are cutting up through a limb and the limb pinches the chain in the top front of the bar, (d) or you are cutting through a limb and contact another limb beyond that one with the kickback zone of the bar.

In any case the front of the bar will be launched upward and back with considerable force and velocity. In severe cases it can dislocate your thumb on the hand that's holding the front bar. I've had saws kick back and the chain ripped the skin off my thumb. Once I nearly lost an eye and ear when the saw kicked back.

To prevent kick-back do not let the tip of the bar and chain contact the wood you are cutting. Keep the wood centered on the bar and don't try to cut trees or limbs that are too large for your saw.

Note: some saws without chain brakes have a safety bar in front of the handle. Its purpose is to deflect the saw should kickback occur. While this is helpful it is not a chain brake. It does nothing to stop the chain.

Chain and Bar Designs

Chain and bar designs improve the performance of your saw and can reduce the chances of kickback.

Homelite
Safe-T-Tip

Homelite (and some other manufacturers) has the most effective anti-kickback feature on the market. They call it the "Safe-T-Tip and it's a shield placed over the end of the bar so that the chain cannot make contact with anything as it screams around the end of the bar. It does make the bar slightly heavier and limits the size of wood you'll be able to cut but the trade-off is virtually no chance of kick-back.

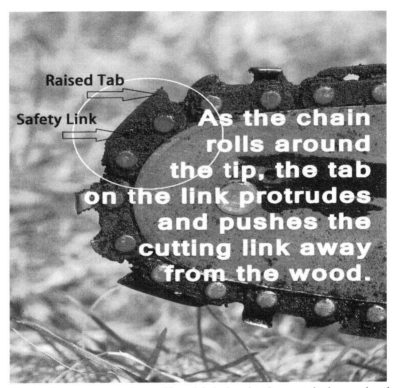

Raised Tab

Safety Link

As the chain rolls around the tip, the tab on the link protrudes and pushes the cutting link away from the wood.

Chain designs can also affect kick-back. One style has raised links between the cutting links on the chain. These often have "tails" on the back end of the link that rise when the chain goes around the tip of the bar and push the cutting edge away from the wood. It's not as fail-safe as the Homelite method but it does help.

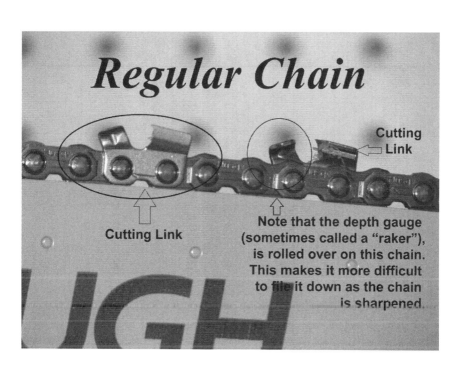

Regular Chain

Cutting Link

Cutting Link

Note that the depth gauge (sometimes called a "raker"), is rolled over on this chain. This makes it more difficult to file it down as the chain is sharpened.

Skip Chain

Cutting Link

Cutting Link

This chain has a raised center link between the cutting links. The raised portion is intended to reduce the chance of kickback.

The "skip-chain" is a fairly recent innovation in chain design. It doesn't prevent kickback but it does improve performance on some saws. It's used on saws that are slightly underpowered for the bar length and is found most often on mini-saws or on larger saws with extended bars.

A skip-chain has fewer cutting links than a "regular" chain. The "standard" chains used on professional saws, have a cutting link on every other link of the chain. A skip chain has a cutting link on every third link.

The skip-chain is less likely to bog down the saw when cutting larger pieces of wood because there aren't as many cutting links in contact as there would be with a regular chain. Because it has less drag, the motor of the saw maintains a higher RPM. This gives the chain more speed so it cuts faster.

It's like going uphill in a big car with a small engine. As you go up the hill the motor slows down and loses power. When the car down-shifts the motor speeds up and the car also speeds up because your engine is in a more efficient power curve. A skip chain keeps your chain saw running in its most efficient power curve for faster cutting.

Large professional saws usually do not have skip-chains. They have enough muscle to power their way through any tree with ease.

The "depth gauges" (sometimes referred to as "depth stops" or "rakers") on a chain are the vertical metal tabs found just in front of the cutting tooth. Some people file these down to give the chain more "bite." If they are filed down too far the chain grabs and jerks the saw as you cut. It also makes kick-back more likely. If the depth stops are too high the chain won't cut well. There are gauges available for measuring the depth gauges. Get one and use it. I usually file them about every third to fifth time I sharpen the chain.

Chapter Four has more information on purchasing and sharpening the chain.

Some chainsaws use springs between the handles and the case to cut down on vibration.

Vibration Dampers

Early saws had steel handles bolted directly to the motor. After a few hours use your hands often became numb from the vibration and frozen from the cold if it was winter time. Then someone got the idea of putting rubber grips or padding on the steel handles. It helped a little on both the cold and vibration problems. Finally somebody thought of attaching the handles with springs or rubber insulators to help dampen vibration from the motor and chain. To that final "somebody" I'd like to say "thanks."

Vibration dampening is the second greatest innovation on modern saws. Vibration dampers not only make chain saws more comfortable to use, they make them safer as well.

It's really difficult to keep control of a chain saw when your hands are numb from vibration. But vibration control is more than a safety issue. You'll be able to spend more time cutting if your saw is comfortable to use.

Oil Pumps

I only mention manual pumps for chain oiling in case you run into an older saw and plan on buying it. I haven't seen a manual chain oil pump in years and I don't miss them. If your chain doesn't get enough oil it will overheat and you will shorten its lifespan. The old manual oilers worked well when used properly but it was not unusual back then to see a lot of bars with sections burned blue from overheated chains. The biggest problem was operator error … the operator forgot to push the plunger to pump oil to the chain!

Saws today have automatic oilers and most function quite well. Some of the better saws have ways to adjust them but even the non-adjustable type I've used worked well as they came from the factory.

The way I check the automatic chain oiler is to point the tip of the bar at the tree or log I'm cutting (keep the chain two or three inches away), and race the engine a couple of times. You should see a "line" of oil spray from the chain on the log. If the automatic oiler isn't working take it in to be repaired. There's probably dirt plugging an orifice somewhere.

Use commercial bar oil. Not used motor oil. Bar oil comes in different weights for winter or summer use. Follow the manufacturers recommended oil weight (viscosity) for your saw.

Electric vs. Gasoline

Electric saws have improved a lot over the years. The new ones are light weight, quiet and powerful, and they don't put out exhaust fumes like gas saws. They have some good things to offer if you have a project near an electrical outlet.

The biggest detriments are that your maximum range is limited by the length of your power cord and they tend to be in the lower power range. If you just want something to do some cutting and trimming around the yard or some minor clean-up of downed limbs after a storm they're worth looking into.

This is a 10 inch, battery powered, Craftsman chainsaw.

I've used a couple of battery powered chainsaws. To say I wasn't impressed would be a huge understatement. The motor/chain speed was slow and battery life was short. I can cut much faster with a hand operated bow saw.

**A 16 inch, Craftsman, electric chainsaw.
At 3.5 horsepower it's capable of
competing against most mini-saws.**

Saws powered by 120 volt household current are another story. The 16 inch Craftsman saw pictured is impressive and will keep up with most gasoline powered mini-saws of the same bar length. The 14 inch McCulloch pictured above also does a good job if the wood isn't too thick.

This is a 14 inch, electric chainsaw manufactured by McCulloch

While I wouldn't recommend an electric chainsaw as your only saw they have some distinct advantages over gas powered saws. If you live in the suburbs where noise limits are enforced an electric saw may be your only option.

Price

Ahh, the bottom line for most of us! In the past year I've seen new gas powered chain saws on sale for $89.99. (I paid $59.00 for my little McCullough Mini-Mac.) I gave almost $400.00 for my Stihl and would have spent even more if I'd had the money to spare. But regardless of the price, most chain saws will last for years with proper care and maintenance.

Now, if you have lots of money there are some very high quality (and expensive) saws in small sizes. But if you plan on buying a bigger saw later and just keep the small one for a spare then you might want to start with a lower priced saw.

Whatever saw you decide on make sure that it fits you well, with a power/size range that you're comfortable with and that you can operate safely.

Chapter Two - Chain Saw Use

Firewood cutting is one of the things I really enjoy about our life-style. The cool, crisp days and brilliant fall colors make working outside a pleasure. Every stick of firewood brings memories of cold winter days spent next to a warm fire as I drink hot cocoa and read one of my favorite books.

But there are some bad memories associated with cutting fire-wood as well. I can testify through personal experience that chainsaws make ragged cuts that cause a great deal of pain and take a long time to heal. I could also tell you about bruises in-flicted by falling trees, logs and limbs. Most of these injuries oc-curred because of improper use of the saw, kickback and fatigue. All of them could have been avoided if I'd known then what I know now.

Safety First!

For starters, always be properly attired when using a chainsaw. Don't have anything dangling around your waist, neck, wrists or any other part of your body. Clothing should allow free move-ment yet not be baggy or loose. Steel-toed boots, chaps, leather gloves and a hard hat are good investments as is comfortable hearing protection. If you have long hair tie it up out of the way.

Always wear safety glasses or some sort of eye protection and ear plugs.

Eliminate distractions. That means no cell phones, radios or music; no thoughts about anything but the task at hand. Leave small children and the dog at home. You don't want junior or Fido running under the tree as it falls to the ground or getting caught by the chain.

Get to know your saw and how to use it safely. Read the owner's manual and this book before you even start your saw.

Stay on the ground when learning to use your saw. After you become proficient on the ground you can try some more challenging methods.

I wish I'd had a video camera the first time I trimmed a large tree. One large limb in particular was hanging low over our driveway so I confidently walked out on the limb, started the saw, and began cutting. Don't get excited, I did not cut off the end I was standing on! However, what I hadn't thought about was what was going to happen when I cut off the other end of the limb. I'd studied up on how to do it so I made the undercut on the limb then began cutting down. The far end began to sag then broke off with a loud "crack."

I was instantly launched upward. I hadn't given a thought to how the limb still attached to the tree would spring upward when I released it from the several hundred pounds of weight that it had been supporting! Sometimes I think my mother should have had the letters "D-U-M-B" tattooed across my forehead!

The good thing was that I kept my footing (I was young back then) and I didn't even drop the saw!

My "friend" who witnessed the act was literally rolling on the ground laughing. If he'd been a little closer I'd have thrown the saw at him!

Ladders are almost as treacherous. Trees sway in the wind. Ladders that are leaning against swaying trees are constantly in motion.

Climbing spikes take a lot of skill as well. They look easy when you see a professional use them but most of those guys could tell about the close calls they've had. They're very dangerous for the novice. If you want to give them a try get some personal instruction from a professional. It's very easy to run one of the spikes through your leg or ankle. They make a large puncture wound that's very painful and takes along time to heal!

Most professionals use "bucket" trucks like those used by the power company to repair power lines. These are obviously much safer than ladders and climbing spikes but you still have to know what you're doing.

So, until you've had some training, keep both feet firmly planted on the ground when using your chainsaw.

Don't push yourself physically. Fatigue is the root cause of many accidents. When you're tired your ability to think clearly is impaired and you may hurry or attempt short cuts that put you in dangerous situations. Compounding the danger, tired muscles don't always react as they should. If you become fatigued, take a break or stop for the day.

Preliminary Inspection

Always give the saw a quick inspection before you start it.

Check the starter rope for fraying around the handle. The most wear usually occurs right below the handle or grip. If the rope is fraying it will look fuzzy or frazzled and be very supple below the pull handle. If the rope has begun to fray but has never broken you might be able to do a quick fix by pulling the rope through the handle and tying it off in a section that isn't frayed. You'll shorten the rope but most of the time there's enough extra length to get away with it one time. Just remember to replace it as soon as you can.

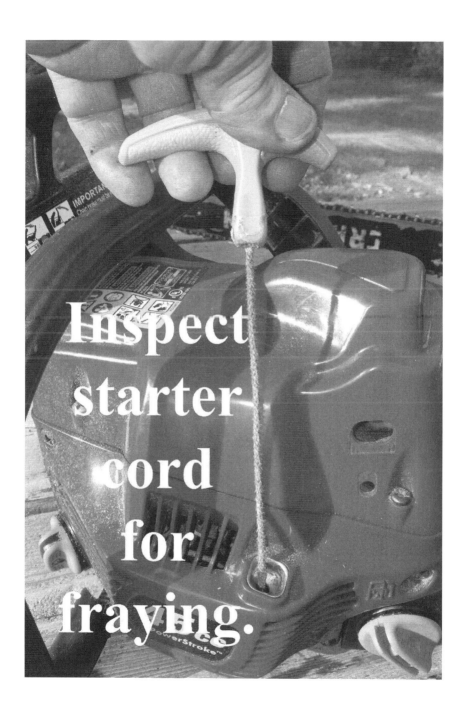

Inspect starter cord for fraying.

Your owner's manual will tell you how to replace the rope for the pull starter. You can buy replacement starting rope from the dealer or go to your local hardware store and purchase rope by the foot for about a third of what the dealer charges. If you go this route, be sure that the rope is strong enough. Many braided ropes look good but they are weak and will break when using them as pull cords. (I learned that the hard way on my snowmobiles.)

Check the saw for broken or loose parts (especially handle mounts). Saws get dropped and things (like trees), get dropped on them. The most common place for them to break is where the handle bolts to the frame. Most handles are rubber or spring mounted now so this problem isn't seen as much as it was in the past but the mounting bolts can work loose over time and the springs or rubber mounts can crack or break so always check them before starting the saw.

Check the saw's case for cracks as well. Most saws use plastic covers for the engine, air filter and starter housing. While you're at it brush the sawdust off the air vents around the recoil starter.

Check the chain brake's operation. Disengage the brake and try rolling the chain around the bar. It should move freely. Now apply the brake. The chain should be held firmly in place. If it isn't then get it fixed.

Inspect the bar and chain. The chain should be sharp. If it isn't go to chapter four and follow the instructions for sharpening the chain. The bar should be straight with no dings, dents or cracks. The groove should not be worn or spread, allowing the chain to roll from side to side. If the rails have feathered edges, remove them with a file. Check for broken cutting teeth on the chain and replace the chain if any are found.

Grease the sprocket through the lube port at the tip of the bar (if it has a lube port - not all bars do!).

Rotate the chain around the bar and check for raised links. If one of the links on the chain rides higher than the others you may have a "ding" or "burr" on the chain's drive link that prevents it from falling into the groove of the bar. If so, take the chain off and file the burr flat and recheck the chain.

If all of the links ride up at the same spot on the bar, the groove on the bar may be pinched. You may be able to fix the bar by carefully prying the pinched spot open with a screwdriver. If not, take it to a repair shop. Often when the groove is pinched the chain will hang-up or be difficult to rotate when the tension is properly set.

Bent or dinged links or missing teeth are usually the result of a chain coming off the bar while you're using the saw. A bent bar or pinched groove on the bar is often due to a tree or large limb pinching the bar while you're cutting. If any of these issues are present you'll probably have recurring problems with the chain coming off the bar.

Also check the bar for burns. Burned sections will look bluish and may smell burned as well. Burning is usually caused by lack of lubrication but may also be caused by a dull or improperly sharpened chain. (If the chain is dull you may compensate by trying to force the bar through the wood. This results in excessive friction and heat where the chain slides through the groove on the bar.)

Chain Tension

Chain tension is set differently depending upon conditions. Generally, if the chain is cold the chain tension should be enough to hold the chain against the bottom of the bar but not so tight that it inhibits its movement around the bar. If the saw is warm the chain can sag somewhat below the bar. Check your owner's manual for your particular saw but in general if the chain sags so far that the flats on the drive links are below the bar's edge then the chain must be tightened.

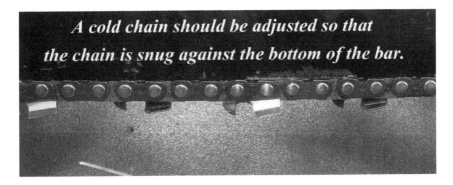

A cold chain should be adjusted so that the chain is snug against the bottom of the bar.

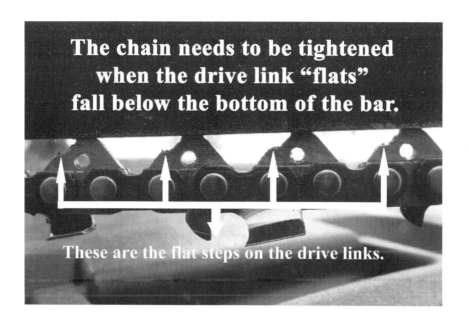

The chain needs to be tightened when the drive link "flats" fall below the bottom of the bar.

These are the flat steps on the drive links.

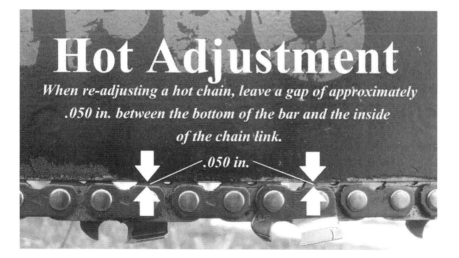

Hot Adjustment

When re-adjusting a hot chain, leave a gap of approximately .050 in. between the bottom of the bar and the inside of the chain link.

.050 in.

Do not over-tighten a hot chain. Leave a little slack (about .050 inch) between the bottom of the bar and the chain. *Note: After you finish cutting for the day loosen up the chain. A hot chain can sometimes contract enough upon cooling to damage the crankshaft.* Be sure to recheck the cold tension the next time you use the saw.

Most chains are adjusted as follows:
   A. Loosen the bolts that hold the sprocket cover. Relax them only enough to allow the bar to slide.
   B. If the saw is cold, tighten the chain adjusting screw until the slack is gone from the bottom of the chain. (The chain should not "sag" below the bar.) If the saw has been in use (hot) then leave a little slack allowing the chain to sag slightly below the bar.
   C. Lift up on the front of the bar and release it then recheck the chain tension.
   D. Tighten the bolts on the sprocket cover and rotate the chain around the bar. The chain should slide easily around the bar. If the chain tension is too tight, go through steps A through D again only don't tighten the chain as much.

If you have an automatic chain oiler check its function by holding the tip of the bar about an inch from a solid surface and racing the chain saw's motor a few times. As the chain rotates around the end of the bar it should throw off drops of oil. This will show up as oil spots in line with the rotating chain. If you don't see any oil after revving the engine five to ten times, take the saw to a repair shop to have it checked.

Finally, check the chain to be sure it's sharp and/or sharpened correctly. If not, sharpen it before you begin cutting. (See chapter four.)

Clean the air filter daily.

Keep a spare spark plug and plug wrench in your tool kit. Spark plugs often fail without warning and it may be a long drive to the parts store. See the owner's manual for recommended service intervals regarding spark plugs and spark arrestors.

Fuel and Bar Oil

Top the fuel tank off with the manufacturer's recommended gaso-
line/oil mixture. We have three saws that require a 40 to 1 mix
and two that use a 50 to 1 mixture. Check the owner's manual to
see if there's a minimum octane rating for fuel and don't go below
it. (No matter what the manufacturer recommends, I always use
premium fuel for my saws.)

If you err on mixing fuel and oil, err on the side of more oil. The
penalty for too much oil is slightly more smoke, slightly de-
creased performance, slightly reduced spark plug life and slightly
more frequent cleaning for the spark arrestor. The penalty for not
using enough oil is a seized motor or greatly reduced engine life.

Quaker State® Universal 2-Cycle Engine Oil for Air-Cooled Engines is a premium formulation designed for hot-running, small, 2-cycle engines such as lawn mowers, chain saws, leaf blowers, string trimmers, edgers, motorcycles and scooters. Suitable for use in either a "premix" or lubricant injection system, it provides good protection against friction, burns cleanly, and helps keep ports clean for maximum output. It also protects ball and needle bearings during high RPM use. Thoroughly mix oil and fuel before use. (JASO FA & FB; API TC)

Mix Oil at Manufacturers' Recommended Ratio

Gas to Oil Ratio	Oil Oz/1 Gal Gas	Oil mL/4 Liters Gas
32:1	4	118
40:1	3.2	95
50:1	2.6	77
100:1	1.3	38

Information: 1-800-BEST OIL
or at www.quakerstate.com

MADE IN U.S.A.
12438   0104

CAUTION: Contains petroleum lubricant. Avoid prolonged or repeated contact with eyes, skin and clothing. Use care when mixing with gasoline. Fuel and fuel vapors are fire and explosion hazards. Do not mix near flame or ignition source. Use with adequate ventilation. Wash thoroughly after handling. KEEP OUT OF REACH OF CHILDREN. For Health Emergencies or Consumer Information call: 1-800-759-2525.

DISTRIBUTED BY SOPUS PRODUCTS, P.O. BOX 4427, HOUSTON, TX 77210-4427
© 2004 SOPUS PRODUCTS

I usually mix the oil a little thicker when using fuel that contains alcohol. Use 2 cycle engine oil designed for mixing with gaso-

line. Never use motor oil, used oil or bar oil for the gas/oil mixture.

Most manufacturers sell small, pre-measured bottles of 2 cycle
oil. They're convenient but you'll pay about four times as much
per ounce of oil as you would if you bought it in quart or gallon
containers and measured it yourself. If you only burn a couple of
gallons of chainsaw gas per year the oil cost is minimal no matter
what size container it comes in. However, if you burn more than
that you might check into purchasing it by the quart or gallon.

One last note regarding mixed fuel: you should clearly label the
gasoline container with the fuel oil mixture. If you put the wrong
gasoline in your 4 cycle mower it will smoke a little and performance may suffer but it will still run without engine damage. Put
the wrong gasoline in your chainsaw and you'll be buying a new
one.

Top off the chain oil tank with bar oil of the proper viscosity
(weight) for the season. Bar oil comes in different "weights" just
like the oil for your vehicle. Refer to the owner manual for the
proper weight for the temperature ranges you'll be working in.
For the longest chain and bar life, it's not recommended that you
use used engine oil to lube the chain due to the impurities it contains and the chance it has picked up dirt and grit.

Starting

Follow the manufacturer's recommendations for starting the saw.
Four of our saws use the following method for a cold start:

1. Set the saw on level ground free of obstructions.
2. Push the primer bulb about ten times.
3. Pull the choke all the way out to the "full choke" position.
4. Lock the throttle on the handle in the full throttle position.
5. Turn the switch on.

6. Place your right foot on the pad at the rear of the saw below the throttle handle. Firmly grip the forward/upper handle with your left hand while pushing down on the handle to hold the saw stationary. Use your right hand to pull the starter rope. Our saws usually start with the second or third pull. If the saw tries to start but quickly dies I usually push the choke half-way in and repeat the process.

Note: Be absolutely sure that the chain will not contact the ground or other obstructions when you pull the starter rope or when the saw starts.

7. When the saw starts, grip the rear/lower handle with your right hand and press the throttle trigger to release the throttle lock. Remove your right foot from the foot pad only after you have the saw firmly under control.

Again, follow the saw manufacturer's recommendation for starting your saw if they differ from those above.

Proper stance for starting the saw.

Proper Cutting Stance

Keep your feet securely planted and maintain a firm grip on the saw at all times. Hold the saw slightly to the side of your body so that if the bar kicks back it will pass harmlessly by your head instead of through it. It's much easier to sew an ear back on than to put the two halves of your head back together.

Keep the area clear of bystanders, pets, brush, limbs, or anything else that will impede your movement or entangle the saw.

Felling (Cutting down a standing tree.)

The hardest I've ever been hit in my life was when I cut down a pine tree with a six-inch trunk. I got careless. It was leaning and the wind was right so I cut straight through the trunk without notching it, (expecting it to fall cleanly to the ground). When the cut was about three inches deep the tree began to fall. Suddenly there was a cracking sound as the trunk barber-chaired. The butt hinged upward then swung to the side and back, right into my stomach. Fortunately I only had the wind knocked out of me and I learned a valuable lesson. Don't be stupid!

Cutting down a tree is normally the most dangerous part of cutting firewood or clearing an area. Even professionals approach this task with caution. When cutting firewood I prefer trees that have already fallen down but if I must cut one down this is how I do it.

First I check to see if the tree is leaning, has more weight (more or larger limbs) on one side, and how straight the trunk is. Generally a tree will fall the direction it leans or to the side that is heaviest.

Most of my cutting is done on mountainsides and the slope can

41

make it difficult to tell the direction a tree leans. I use a plumb line to determine lean. I tie a weight (a nut, sinker, rock, etc.) to the end of a string that's about twelve to twenty-four inches long. I then hold the other end of the string up high and let the weight straighten out the string. The string is now absolutely vertical. I use the string as a reference to indicate which direction the tree is leaning. If there's a lot of weight on one side or the tree leans very far in one direction you must be extra cautious when felling it.

Remember, it's best to drop a tree in the direction it naturally wants to fall. Leave the challenging projects to the experts.

The next thing I check is the wind. It's best to have no wind or a light, steady breeze. If the wind is strong or swirling wait for a better day to drop that tree.

Again, don't try to drop a tree against the wind. Leave that job to the experts.

If there's a strong wind or the tree has a lot of extra weight on one side, or is leaning you have a good recipe for a condition called a "barber chair."

Barber Chairs and Rocking Chairs

A barber chair occurs when a tree falls and the trunk begins to

43

split vertically. This creates a hinge that may extend several feet above the cut you've made. The danger here is that when the tree falls the base will rise into the air and slam backwards or to the side with deadly force. Obviously you don't want this to happen to you.

What causes a tree to barber chair is an excessive amount of weight (or force from high winds) on one side. As you cut through the trunk the tension increases on the remaining wood until the tree falls. Normally the fall begins slowly and builds momentum as the tree falls farther toward the ground. When a tree barber chairs, the wood builds up tension until it suddenly snaps and the tree falls. If your notch isn't deep enough the tree trunk may splinter, creating a "hinge" at a point several feet above the cut. As the tree falls to the ground the butt pivots up until the splintered section can no long hold the weight of the tree. At that point the trunk breaks free and falls to the ground. Unfortunately, you don't know which way it's going to fall or where it will land.

This is the perfect recipe for creating a "barber chair."

The tree is leaning which puts a great deal of tension on the back side.

Trees fall when the fibers are stretched beyong their breaking point. At that time it's like a thousand small tendons and ligaments all break at once.

High wind or a tree that has a preponderance of limbs or weight on one side have the same potential to create a "barber chair" as when a tree leans one direction.

The felling cut is the correct height above the notch's bottom cut but due to the tree's lean there's trouble ahead!

Note that the notch is much too shallow.

45

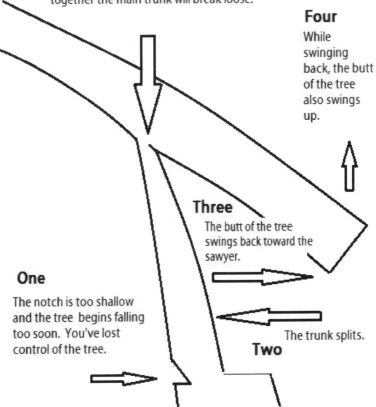

Five

The split portion of the tree narrows as it proceeds up
the trunk. When it gets too weak to hold the tree
together the main trunk will break loose.

Four

While
swinging
back, the butt
of the tree
also swings
up.

Three

The butt of the tree
swings back toward the
sawyer.

One

The notch is too shallow
and the tree begins falling
too soon. You've lost
control of the tree.

The trunk splits.

Two

The split has continued up the tree where it will come to a point. When the weight of the trunk is too much the butt end of the tree will come crashing down.

The top of the tree has headed to earth which raised the butt of the log high in the air.

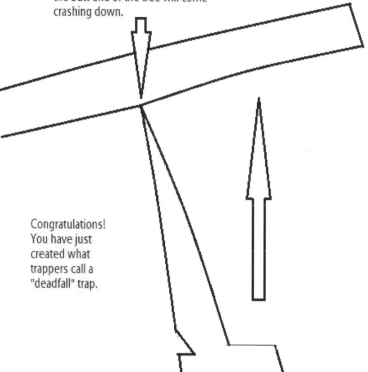

Congratulations! You have just created what trappers call a "deadfall" trap.

The main trunk has broken loose. At this point the only thing you know for sure is that it is going down. It may twist to one side or the other. It may go backward (most likely), or forward (least likely), or it may twist and roll. If may throw off splinters of wood large enough to skewer you. You just don't know what's going to happen next.

In any case your best defense is to get as far away as you can and get something large and solid between you and it!

Always have several escape paths cleared before you start cutting.

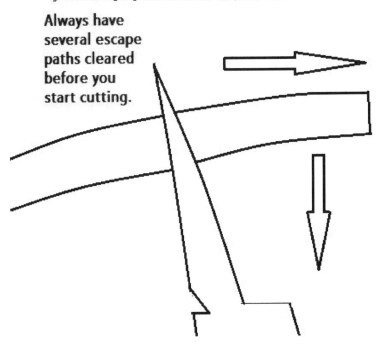

There are several ways of cutting the tree down to reduce the risk of a barber chair but the key word here is "reduce." They do not eliminate that possibility. The best advice is to leave those trees to the professionals. I won't cut one down unless there's no other option.

Another danger inherent in the tree itself is what I call a "rocking chair." This is a condition in which the tree's trunk is shaped like the rocker of a wooden rocking chair or the keel of a boat. When the tree falls the base may rock high into the air and then roll to one side or the other. Again, if there's anything of value (like you!) standing in the way the consequences could be disastrous.

Estimating Height

Once I've evaluated the direction of lean, weight distribution, rocking chair and wind direction and have a fair idea of which way this tree wants to fall I check for space. (You don't want the tree to fall on power lines, buildings, vehicles, fences, people, other trees or your pick-up!)

A stick can be used to estimate the height of a tree.

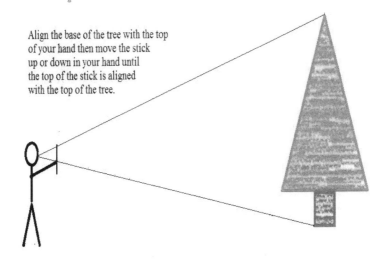

Align the base of the tree with the top of your hand then move the stick up or down in your hand until the top of the stick is aligned with the top of the tree.

Step back from the tree and hold the stick at arm length and parallel to the tree's trunk. The distance you step away from the tree will depend on terrain and the size of the tree. The farther away from the tree you are - within reason! - the more accurate this will be.

Sight down your arm and raise/lower your arm until your thumb is at the base of the tree.

Now, hold your arm in place while you twist your wrist ninety-degrees so that the stick is now parallel with the ground.

Sight across the end of the stick to get an estimate of where the top of the tree will land when it falls.

Without moving your arm, slide the stick up or down through your hand until the top of the stick is the same height as the tree. Now, your arm should be straight with the stick in a vertical position with your thumb at the base of the tree and the top of the stick even with the top of the tree.

Now pivot your arm ninety degrees to the direction of fall. With your thumb still marking the base of the tree the tip of the stick will be aligned with the point where the top will land.

Ropes and Cables

Some people use ropes and cables to aid in the direction of a tree's fall. Note that I said aid in the direction of fall. Don't try to use cables to make a tree go where it doesn't want to fall. Leave such jobs to professionals. I've seen four-wheel-drive-pickups dragged with all four wheels sliding by trees that didn't fall the direction intended.

51

Climb the tree to fasten the rope (or use a ladder or ladder truck) then anchor the other end to a solid object. I prefer anchoring to another tree and using a cable hoist (come-along) to apply some tension. Note that I said "some" tension. Don't try to pull the tree over with the cable! If you need that much pull then you're doing something wrong! Keep bystanders away from the cable. If it breaks it can snap back with deadly force. Always, be safety conscious.

Assuming that there's a reasonable expectation for the tree to fall safely in the direction you need it to go it's now time to fire up the chainsaw.

Notches and Wedges

Begin the felling process by making a notch in the tree on the side you want the tree to fall. Make your first cut downward at a 45 degree or steeper angle until you've gone about one-third of the distance through the trunk. Make the next cut parallel to the ground so that it intersects the bottom of the first cut. Knock the loose piece of wood free if it hasn't fallen away already. Now begin cutting horizontally from the opposite side of the tree (the direction away from the fall). This cut should be about one third of the height of the notch above the horizontal cut made for the notch. For example: if the open end of the notch is six inches then the second cut should be about two inches above the flat portion of the notch. If the notch's open side measures nine inches then the second cut should be about three inches higher than the flat cut in the notch.

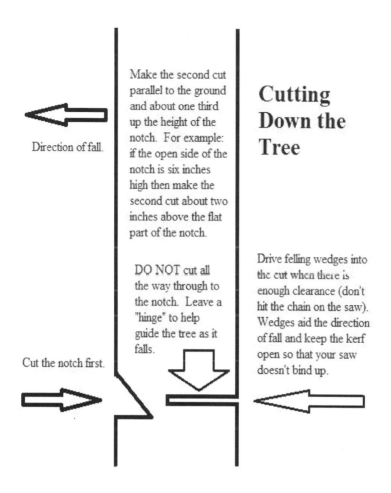

Cutting Down the Tree

Direction of fall.

Make the second cut parallel to the ground and about one third up the height of the notch. For example: if the open side of the notch is six inches high then make the second cut about two inches above the flat part of the notch.

DO NOT cut all the way through to the notch. Leave a "hinge" to help guide the tree as it falls.

Cut the notch first.

Drive felling wedges into the cut when there is enough clearance (don't hit the chain on the saw). Wedges aid the direction of fall and keep the kerf open so that your saw doesn't bind up.

CAUTION: Before you cut the notch check the tree for signs of decay. Be especially cautious of trees with multiple holes bored by woodpeckers (birds) in the trunk or trees with round holes in the trunk that are the entrances to animal and bird dens. Assuming that there are no obvious signs of decay cut the notch. While you are cutting the notch, be aware of the type of sawdust you generate. If it's powdery the tree may have a rotten core. You should either stop cutting or proceed very carefully. This tree could fall at any time and you may not be able to control its direction.

If the bottom part of the trunk is good but there are decayed sections higher up the tree may break apart as it falls or when it hits the ground. The danger here is that you don't know where the broken sections are going to go.

When you make the final cut it's a good idea to drive in one or more felling wedges as the saw makes its way through the tree.

DO NOT USE steel wedges made for splitting firewood. Felling wedges are made out of plastic or wood so that they won't damage the chain. These are especially helpful for those trees that stand straight up, to give them a nudge in the right direction. I've had well balanced trees collapse straight down on the saw when I cut through the "hinge" section (never a good idea!). At that point I didn't know which direction the tree would fall. Felling wedges would have started the tree in the direction I wanted it to go.

Top: Home made felling wedge.
Bottom: Commercial plastic wedge.

Wedges aren't needed as often on trees with a slight lean to them. (Uhmm, did I mention that you should never try to drop a tree against the direction it leans?)

Keep an eye on the top of the tree as you cut. A half inch movement at the saw cut may be twenty feet of movement at the top of the tree. Which do you think is easier to see? By watching the top of the tree you'll be able to discern the direction of fall quicker, plus, you can tell if the wind has changed or if the tree is beginning to twist as it falls.

DO NOT CUT INTO THE NOTCH. If you do you've lost control of the tree as it falls. Leave a "hinge" to help guide the tree in the right direction as it falls.

As soon as the tree begins its fall get to a safe place. I always clear limbs and brush away from the tree and have at least two escape plans in place before I cut the notch. Again my favorite refuge is behind a nearby tree that's large enough to deflect the tree I'm cutting should something go wrong. If I can't find a tree large enough I'll have several cleared paths to get away from the tree as far and fast as I can.

Once the tree's on the ground it's time to whittle it down to firewood size.

Spring-poles

A "spring-pole" is a limb or smaller tree that's pinned or held under tension by the tree you just dropped. Always remember that any limb held by another tree or the ground could be under a tremendous amount of tension and may break with explosive force as you cut through it. Whenever possible keep the main trunk between you and the limb you are cutting.

Trimming/Limbing/Bucking

I start with limbs that aren't touching any solid object. It's best to whittle large limbs down a piece at a time from the far ends rather than cut them off at the trunk. Smaller sections are less likely to cause harm than when cutting off a branch that may weigh several hundred pounds. Be aware of any shifting of the tree's trunk as you cut. Some limbs may be large enough that the trunk could shift or roll as the extra weight is removed.

Any limb that's touching the ground or another tree or limb may, like the kick-stand on a bicycle, be holding the tree's trunk in position. When you cut through it the trunk may roll or it may spring backwards. Look things over before you cut and be ready to move out of the way at the first hint of danger.

Cutting Up, Cutting Down

I'm willing to bet that anyone who's cut a lot of wood has pinched the bar at least once. A pinched bar occurs when you are cutting through a log or limb and it bends, pinching the saw in the kerf (the groove the saw makes in the wood). You can avoid this by cutting either up or down depending on how the limb is supported.

If the log is supported at the ends and you are cutting between the supports, gravity is going to make it sag as you cut through it. The proper way to cut would be to begin at the bottom and cut upward through the limb or log. That way, as it sags it will open the kerf instead of closing it.

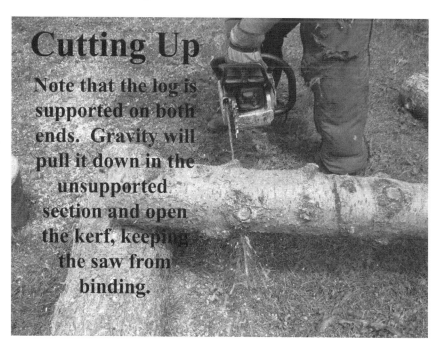

Cutting Up
Note that the log is supported on both ends. Gravity will pull it down in the unsupported section and open the kerf, keeping the saw from binding.

If you are cutting beyond the last place the limb or log is supported so that the end you are cutting will fall down then begin your cut at the top and cut down. As you cut, the end will sag and open the kerf.

Cutting Down

The end of the log is not supported so it will be best to cut down from the top. That way gravity will pull the kerf open as the saw cuts through the log.

You should always have an extra saw or ax in case you need to free a pinched saw. If your saw is pinched use another saw to make a cut next to and parallel to the first cut but from the opposite direction. If I'm cutting alone I usually bring an extra chain saw along just in case I pinch my main saw. You can also free a pinched saw by using an ax to cut the wood from either side of the pinched bar. Just be careful that you don't hit your saw with the ax.

Kickback

One final note on safety. There is a condition called kickback that occurs when the front, of the bar and chain comes into contact with a solid object while the chain is spinning. It's like raising a car on a jack, starting it up and putting it into gear, then, once the wheels are spinning, letting the jack down. The car will shoot forward as the wheels contact the ground.

This is what happens in kickback. The chain is spinning around the front of the nose sprocket when it makes contact with a solid object. However, instead of stopping the chain the front of the bar is launched upward with tremendous force. Now, the pivot point on the chain saw is the back grip. The end of the bar is going to do its best to rotate around this axis and saw through anything that stands in the way. Including you!

Kickback is most likely to occur (1) when cutting up through a limb or trunk using the tip of the bar, (2) when cutting down through a limb and the tip of the bar is pinched in the kerf, or (3) when you are cutting through a limb and the tip of the bar makes contact with an object on the other side of the log you are cutting.

Be aware when using your saw. This is a perfect set-up for kickback.

Do Not let the tip of your saw contact any other object when cutting.

Chain brakes will usually stop the chain but not the bar. You can still get some nasty injuries so don't get sloppy hoping the chain brake will save you from harm. I always wear a hard hat and hold the saw to the side so that if kickback does occur the bar will pass beside my head instead of directly through it.

The most important thing to do is to walk away if you feel a job is beyond your present abilities. There's no shame in passing up a tree that may get you or someone else killed or seriously injured. If it's a tree that must be cut and you aren't sure you can handle it then call in a professional.

Hopefully you'll learn from my mistakes and have a safe, enjoyable time in the woods.

Chapter Three - Chain Saw Maintenance

Many chainsaw problems can be traced directly to poor or improper maintenance. I've already covered some maintenance issues in the previous chapter under the section titled, "Preliminary Inspection."

Most chainsaws come with a wrench to change the spark plug and chain. You'll find that over time you'll accumulate a few more items. I carry the tools and equipment to sharpen the chain and do minor repairs on the saw when away from home. This includes Allen wrenches, pliers and specialty screwdrivers. You should always have a spare spark plug and cutting chain on hand. Spark plugs can fail at any time under use and if you hit a rock you may ruin a chain in less than a second. I keep everything in a small tool box that I take directly to the woods when I'm cutting firewood.

I always keep one saw ready for use. I drain the gasoline and chain oil reservoir at the end of the season but I keep one gallon of fresh fuel (with fuel stabilizer if needed) and a premixed bottle of oil ready. That way if a storm moves through and I need the saw to clear downed trees or limbs I can have it running with minimal effort.

I replace the spark plug at the end of the season unless it fails before then. Some manufacturers suggest replacing the spark plug after 50 hours of use. See your manual for specifics.

Chains are inspected daily and sharpened or changed as needed. I often keep worn chains around for cutting out stumps. I almost always dig the chain into the ground at one point when cutting out a stump so I use old chains for that task.

Turn the bar over every other time you install a new chain so that it will wear evenly. Yes, you'll get some funny looks from less knowledgeable onlookers who'll give you a hard time about the bar being upside down but you'll get longer life from the bar if you rotate it frequently.

The most common reason for a chain to come off the bar (assuming it is adjusted correctly) is a worn or bent bar. If the chain groove is tapered or too shallow the chain will slip out of it under load or at high chain speeds. By rotating the bar you'll wear both sides evenly. If you wait until there's noticeable wear on the bottom of the bar and then rotate it, you're too late.

Inspect the drive sprocket for wear. If it's worn grooves where the drive links ride then replace the sprocket.

Inspect the drive sprocket for wear and replace if necessary.

If it has a "roller nose" sprocket at the front of the bar inspect it and the bar for wear.

I usually clean the spark arrestor and muffler at the end of the season but it may need it more often depending upon conditions. They sometimes accumulate carbon deposits that restrict the exhaust flow. When this happens the saw becomes "sluggish." The motor will accelerate slowly and seem underpowered. Again, see the owner's manual for recommended service intervals.

Storing Your Saw

Long term storage is defined differently depending upon the

manufacturer. Some define "long term" as any period thirty-days or more in which you won't be using your saw. Others stretch that to three months. In our case I prepare our saws for storage at the end of the season when my wood shed is full.

It doesn't take long to prepare a saw for storage or to put it back in action when you need it but if you store your saw improperly it may take hours or a trip to the shop to get it going the next time you need it.

The first thing to do is swish the fuel around in the tank then dump it. Inspect the tank for debris. If you see any then pour some clean fuel in the tank and repeat the process. Once the tank is clean (and empty) start the saw and run it until it quits. You want the carburetor to be dry so that the diaphragm(s) don't get sticky. Empty the bar oil reservoir.

Always recycle or dispose of oil and gasoline in an environmentally safe manner.

Now give the saw a general clean-up and inspection. Repair or replace any worn sprockets, bars, chains, pull cords, or other parts. Clean or replace the air filter as needed. Change the spark plug (if needed – see the owner's manual). Clean the muffler and spark arrester and be sure to clean the nooks and crannies around the chain brake and sprocket.

Some manufacturer's recommend that you remove the chain, clean it and put it in a covered pan of oil for storage. I've never found this to be necessary but if you live where there's a lot of humidity or the saw may be stored for an extended period, it's probably a good idea. In my case I make sure the chain is clean, oil it with bar oil, then re-install it on the bar.

While the chain is off I grease the roller nose in the bar while turning the roller sprocket to distribute the grease all the way around (be sure to lube both sides).

At this point I put the bar and chain back on the saw and put it in storage. Leave the chain just a little bit loose (let it sag slightly under the bar). I always store the saw in its case or (if it doesn't have a case) I cover the bar it's full length with a chain and bar cover. Store the saw in a clean, dry area.

All I have to do to put the saw to work is add gasoline, fill the oil reservoir, adjust the chain, and start the saw.

Don't try to save the mixed fuel too long. The time will vary according to how you store it. It degrades rapidly. If you want to have fuel on hand (a practice I recommend) fill a gas can and add a gasoline preservative to the fuel. Keep a pre-measured bottle of oil in the tool kit and when you need the saw all you have to do is dump the oil into the fuel and mix it up and you're ready to go.

I always keep fuel on hand for emergency use. If a windstorm, tornado, or ice or snowstorm roll through (or any other disaster) you may not be able to get to a gasoline station. If the power is out then they won't be pumping gas anyway and you may need your saw to clear fallen trees or broken limbs or to cut some firewood to heat your home. A chain saw can be a very good investment even if you never use it to cut firewood. Keep yours in good shape and ready for use at all times.

Chapter Four - Chain Purchasing and Sharpening

I'd gone out to the wood lot to see why our son was taking so long to cut through the tree he was working on. We'd just bought a brand new saw so the older boys could help with the firewood cutting. I'd dropped the tree and instructed the oldest on how to cut it up. It was a small tree and he should have been done by now. He had to be getting low on gasoline so I picked up the cans of gas and oil and trudged the hundred yards to where he was cutting. When I topped the rise I could see him rocking the saw as if the chain was dull. I sighed deeply and growled inwardly, thinking he must have hit a rock with the saw and dulled the chain.

When I got to him I motioned for him to shut off the saw. I expected to give him some grief over hitting a rock and dulling a brand new chain but when I inspected the chain it didn't have a dull tooth on it. I fired it up and tried cutting. The saw made very little progress so I pushed down hard to make it cut faster. It still wouldn't cut. In fact, it didn't seem to faze the saw at all. That was strange because it should have bogged the motor down. Plus, the "sawdust" it spewed looked more like dust than the thin ribbons of wood that should have been generated by a sharp chain.

I shut it off and we took it to the shop for further inspection. The problem was that the factory chain was very poorly sharpened. It was most likely by intent to insulate them from a lawsuit because some moron cut himself and tried to sue the company. Every cutting tooth appeared sharp but the angle was way too shallow and they'd left the depth gauges on the chain so high that the teeth barely contacted the wood.

I quickly removed the factory chain and installed the spare chain that we'd bought at the same time we purchased the saw. That one cut perfectly. I put the factory chain aside for a rainy day when I'd have time to sharpen it correctly. We were burning daylight and there was still wood to be cut.

Saw Chain Basics

There are literally hundreds of different chain styles or designs. When you purchase a chain at a discount store you'll likely have very few options to choose from (the store manager has done that for you). There's nothing inherently wrong with that but if you go to a saw shop or order your saw chain online you'll need to understand some of the differences you'll encounter.

Rip, Crosscut, Artistic

Saw chains fall into one of three categories: ripping, crosscut, or carving (artistic).

Ripping chains are specialty chains designed for cutting lengthwise with the wood's grain. These are recommended if you use a chainsaw type lumber mill to cut trees into boards or lumber. I'm not going into a lot of detail on rip chains. If you're only ripping a few boards or planks or squaring off a few logs for a building project you probably don't need to invest in a rip chain. If you do, visit your local chainsaw shop or order one online.

Artistic chains are for chainsaw carvers. These people use

chainsaws to cut statues or figures out of tree trunks or make other types of "art" out of large sections of trees. (They also have special carving bars for their saws.) It's a relatively specialized market so if you're into it then visit a saw shop or order them online. I'm not going to say any more because the focus of this book is on firewood cutting.

The type of chain you're most likely to use are crosscut chains. These are used for cutting across the grain of the tree as when felling a tree or cutting one up for firewood.

Low-Kickback vs. Aggressive

Saw Chain is also graded in degrees of aggressiveness. Generally, the more aggressive a chain is the faster it will cut through the wood. You can control this to a degree when sharpening the chain. If you file the depth gauge links below recommended clearances the cutting links will dig deeper into the wood and cut faster. The downside to doing this is the saw will lurch and grab as you make the cut and the saw may bog down easier. The second concern is that you greatly increase the chances of kickback.

Most home-owner saws come with less aggressive chains to reduce chances of kickback. These chains cut well as long as you stay with trees that are shorter than the flat or straight side of the bar but if you cut trees wide enough that the nose of the bar is cutting as well these chain will slow you down. In some instances these chains will not cut at all at the curved part of the bar's tip.

I've posted some photos showing different chains rated as aggressive or low kickback. Study them to see why each has earned it's rating.

This is another example of a skip chain.
The raised links between the cutting links
make it less likely to kick back while cutting.

This is a low-kickback chain.

Note how the ear on the raised link pushes
the bar away from the wood at the tip.

This chain is also a low-kickback chain because it
has raised links between the cutting links.
Note how the raised links push the bar away from the
wood being cut as they round the end of the bar.

This is a standard chain on a professional saw.
It has no provisions to prevent kickback.

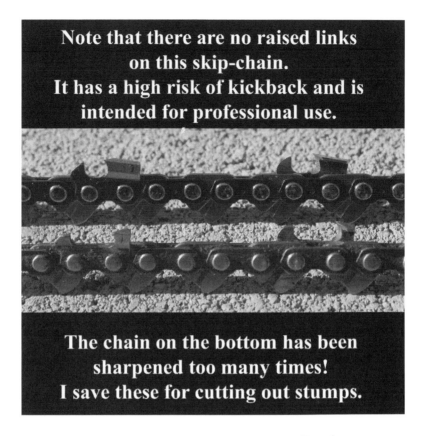

Note that there are no raised links
on this skip-chain.
It has a high risk of kickback and is
intended for professional use.

The chain on the bottom has been
sharpened too many times!
I save these for cutting out stumps.

Understanding links, pitch, gauge, kerf and file size

Your choices when purchasing saw chain at your local hardware
or discount store will probably be limited. They'll stock chain
that most closely matches what the manufacturer installed on the
saws. That's not necessarily a problem but if you go to a saw
shop you may find yourself confused by some of the choices
you'll have.

We've already mentioned the three main types of saw chain
(cross-cut, ripping and artistic) and we've seen some of the
differences between low-kickback chains intended for
homeowners and aggressive chains intended for professional use.

Now we'll look at some of measurements you'll want to know (and understand!) when purchasing saw chain.

In order to purchase a chain that fits there are three things you must know: pitch, gauge, and the number of links. To sharpen the chain you'll need to know what size of file to purchase. And you should at least know what is meant by "kerf."

Pitch is the measurement of how close together the links are on the chain. It's determined by measuring across three chain rivets then dividing that number in half.

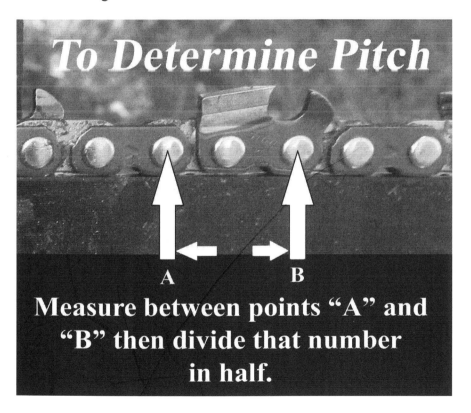

To Determine Pitch

Measure between points "A" and "B" then divide that number in half.

"Gauge" refers to the thickness of the drive link. For this you'll need machinist grade dial or vernier calipers or a micrometer.

Gauge Measurement

Measure the thickness of the Drive Link.

Number of "**Drive Links**." Sorry! There are no shortcuts here. You have to count them!

File Size (No, I'm not talking about megabytes!)

Some information you'll simply have to get from the
manufacturer and file size is one of them. Most manufacturer's
print the information on the box the chain came in. If it's not on
the box then ask the retailer what size file you need. As you'll see
in the section on sharpening your chain, file size is crucial to
getting your chain sharp so be sure you have the right
information.

Kerf and other miscellaneous information.

The "kerf" is the width of the groove the chain cuts. In most
cases you won't have much choice and most of the time it really
doesn't matter. A narrower kerf takes less horsepower simply
because you're cutting a smaller volume of wood. The down side
is that it's easier for the saw to get bound up if the kerf is narrow.
Most professional saws have a wide kerf. They have the power to
handle the extra horsepower needed and you'll experience fewer

problems with the saw binding up when cutting a wider kerf.

Other options you might see on a chain selection guide include low profile, chisel shape, low vibration, carbide cutters, and numerous others including extremely tough chains designed for rescue work by fire departments and other emergency service organization.

Like I've said before, if you purchase your chain at a hardware or discount store your options will be limited. That's not necessarily bad. It just means the merchant has chosen the types most suited to his customers. If you go to a professional saw shop ask them for advice. They'll primarily be looking at your experience, the type/size of saw you use, and what you'll be cutting with it.

Sharpening the Chain

While sharpening the chain isn't rocket science it does need to be done right for safe and efficient cutting. There are so-called, "self-sharpening," and "carbide" chains available but even they will need to be sharpened eventually. If you only use your saw sporadically you can probably get by with having the chain sharpened professionally. I've even know people who just threw away the old chain when it dulled and bought a new one. It doesn't have to be that way.

When to Sharpen

The first things I notice when my chain needs sharpened is that the saw cuts crooked and/or I find myself pushing down on the saw or rocking it back and forth like a rocking chair to make a cut. (*Note: a worn or bent bar will also make the saw cut crooked.*) Sometimes I'll see a bunch of sparks and realize that I hit a rock. I usually have a few choice words to say about idiot chainsaw operators when that happens.

But you don't have to hit a rock to dull a chain (although that will certainly do a fine job of it!). Chains, like any other cutting implement will dull with use. Trees collect a very fine, sandpaper-like layer of dust and dirt that's just waiting to take the edge off your chain. When you drop a tree it picks up grit from the ground and if you drag a tree you rub dirt and sand into the wood. Even squirrels and birds deposit abrasive materials. So even if you're careful when cutting you're eventually going to have to deal with a dull chain so it's a good idea to know how to sharpen it.

The Cutting Edge

To properly sharpen a chain you must first understand how they work. The photos show a chainsaw's cutting tooth. Some angles are built into the tooth. Looking down (Photo One) you'll notice two things of importance. First is the side relief angle. This is built into the chain and is necessary to get a clean cut and to reduce drag on the chain. Angle "A" is the actual cutting angle filed into the tooth. It doesn't have to be a perfect 30 degree angle (anywhere from 25 to 45 degrees seems to work okay) but it must be the same for every tooth.

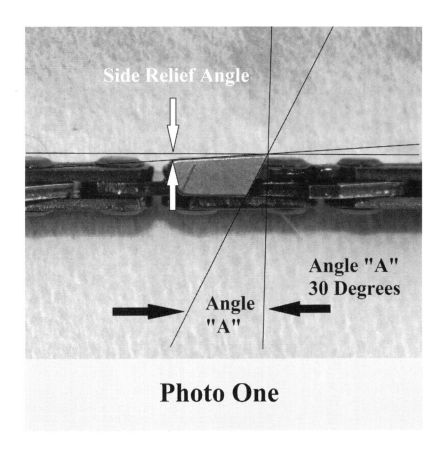

Photo One

Looking at the chain from the side view (Photo Two) you'll observe that it's higher at the front than at the rear of the cutting tooth. This is the top relief angle and it's there for the same reason as the side relief angle, to reduce drag and cut cleaner.

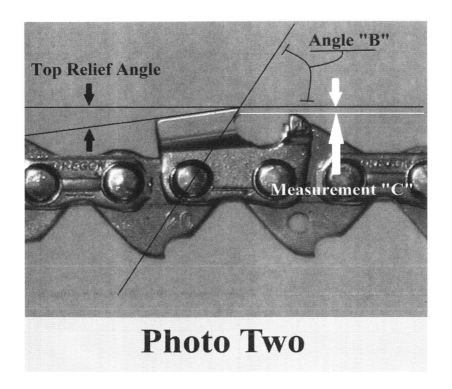

Photo Two

Note angle "B" and measurement "C." As measured from the side, the top cutting edge (angle "B") should be about 15 to 30 degrees from vertical. The more vertical this cutting edge is, the less aggressive it will cut. A less aggressive chain reduces the chance of kickback but it cuts slower. A more aggressive (35 degrees) cutting edge cuts faster but increases the chances of kickback. Until you have some experience using a chainsaw I'd recommend following the chain manufacturer's recommended angles. As noted above, every tooth must be sharpened at the same angle.

Depth gauge clearance is shown in "C." Again, you can modify it somewhat according to your cutting situation. A wider gap will make the chain bite and grab more but it will cut faster. A narrower gap will give a smoother, slower cut. Generally if you're cutting green or soft wood you can get away with a slightly wider gap. If you're cutting seasoned or hard wood you'll want a narrower gap. Be careful here. It's better to have too little gap than too much. A small change in gap makes a big difference when cutting. If in doubt stay with the chain manufacturer's recommendation.

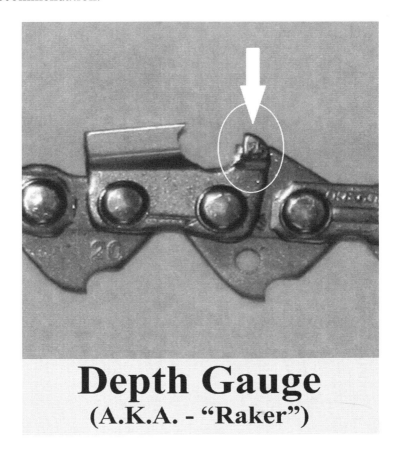

Depth Gauge
(A.K.A. - "Raker")

When you file down the depth gauge teeth you should round off the leading edge for smoother cutting.

Tools

The only tools absolutely necessary to sharpen a chain is a chain file and a flat file but there are some accessories that can make the job easier.

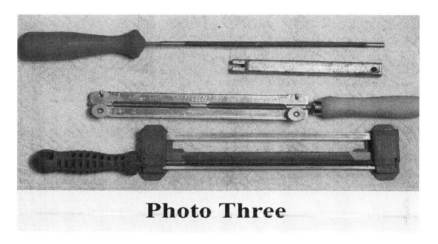

Photo Three

My favorites are the tools pictured in photo 3.

The bottom tool is manufactured by Husqvarna. It has degree markings for angle "A," a rod to set the correct depth for angle "B" and also has a flat file attached that will file down the depth gauges as you sharpen the chain.

The second tool has degree markings on the top to help set the proper angle "A" (see illustration) for your stroke. The file fits into a groove in the jig so that the file will be at the proper depth in the cutting tooth to give you the most efficient cutting angle "B."

I sometimes use the third tool (a "jointer" - for setting depth gauges) about every third to fifth time I sharpen the chain. The rest of the time I use a file, simply because it takes less time.

You can buy sharpening jigs that clamp to the bar and they work great. They take longer to set up but will give you professional results every time. There are tools you can use with a dremel-type tool or drill to sharpen chains. They consist of a small grindstone with a guide to set the angle and depth of cuts. They are fast but in my experience wear out quickly. Plus, as the stone wears it also becomes smaller which cuts the wrong angle "B" (see photo two).

Sharpening Procedure

The easiest way to sharpen a chain is to clamp the chainsaw's bar in a vise with the vise's jaws in the solid, center portion of the bar. (If I'm in the woods I'll brace the bar against a tree stump or other solid object and do the best I can.) Next tighten the chain tension until it's difficult to rotate the chain around the bar. This helps keep the chain from moving around as you file it. Now position the file as shown in photo 4 (approximately 30 degrees) keeping at a 90 degree angle to the bar. Make a full, smooth stroke with the file while maintaining your angles. Count the number of strokes you make and use the same number on every tooth.

Remember, files cut in one direction only. You need to remove the file at the end of the cutting stroke, move the file back, then stroke it forward again for the next cut.

The reason for using the same number of strokes is to keep all of the teeth at the same height. As you noticed in the illustration, the top of the teeth slant towards the back (top relief angle). As you sharpen the chain the cutting tooth gets lower and narrower. If the teeth are not sharpened equally the higher teeth will dig deeper and the lower teeth will just skim the surface. The chain will jerk and cut slower. The same thing is happening at the side of the tooth because of the side angle relief. The wider teeth will grab and the narrower teeth will skim the surface. Also, uneven sharpening is the main cause of crooked cutting and the bar getting bound up in the wood because of the curve in the cut. Take your time and do it right. It'll save a lot of headaches!

Note: be absolutely sure that you have the correct size file. You'll never get angle "B" correct if the file is too big or small. Never use a "rat-tail" file. Use only files made for chain sharpening. After you've sharpened all of the teeth you'll need to check the depth gauges. There are gauges you can purchase for this job or you can use a straight-edge of some type. I often use a straight edge (a square steel rod about six-inches long). At the center of the bar I lay the straight edge across the top of the teeth. I then slide a .025 feeler gauge between it and the depth gauge. If it drags or won't slide through I use a flat file to file the depth gauge down a little and check again. Repeat the process until you have the proper depth.

If you use a commercial gauge (jointer - see photo 3) you just lay it across the teeth with the slot over the depth gauge (AKA – Raker) tooth . If the tooth extends above the slot, remove the tool and file the depth gauge down. Recheck until the depth gauge tooth is below the top surface of the tool's slot.

Unless you took a lot off the chain sharpening it you should only need to file depth gauges every third to fifth time you sharpen the chain.

**A properly sharpened chain will cut
long "ribbons" of wood ... not "dust."**

The Proof is in the Cutting

Now that you've sharpened the chain, re-adjust the chain tension and give it a test run. A properly sharpened chain should cut straight and smooth, without grabbing and without a need to push or rock the saw. It should slice through the wood…not grind through.

If your sharpening efforts weren't too successful the first time read through this chapter again and give it another shot. Take your time and concentrate on getting the angles right. It's one of those things that gets easier with practice.

Chapter Five – Best Woods for the Woodpile

I'm kind of picky about the wood I cut because I want to get the best value for my time and energy. One of the first things you'll notice when heating with wood is that all wood is not created equal. Some burn hotter and longer, some are easy to split while others are extremely difficult. Some kinds leave so much ash you have to shovel out the firebox almost daily and others leave almost no residue behind. When it comes to filling my wood shed, I want wood that's seasoned, easy to split, burns hot (preferably without throwing out a lot of sparks), and leaves very little ash behind. If it's easy to get that's just an added bonus.

If you purchase your firewood from a vendor, knowing which woods are best is even more important. Locally the price for a cord of wood varies considerably depending upon the type of wood, whether it's split or in the round, if it's in log lengths, and whether or not it's seasoned. It's helpful to know if Larch firewood at $100.00 per cord is a better buy than White Pine at $90.00 per cord. In order to determine this you'll need to know the heat value of the wood when dry, how long the wood has been seasoned, if it's split or "in the round," and how much wood is in a "cord."

Heat Value

When woodcutters get together and discuss which wood is the "best" they're usually referring to the heat value of the wood itself. Heat value is commonly measured by BTU's (British Thermal Units). One BTU is the amount of energy needed to increase the temperature of one pound of water one degree Fahrenheit at a constant pressure of one atmosphere (the air pressure at sea level).

In the spreadsheet you'll see the heat value of one cord of wood expressed in Million BTU's. *Note: These are for comparisons only. When I did the research there were often discrepancies between labs due to factors such as moisture content, the actual cubic feet of wood per cord, and different testing methods.*

BTU ratings are based on a full, 128 cubic foot, cord of wood. That's a stack of wood measuring four feet high, four feet wide and eight feet long. However, the actual volume of wood in a cord will vary depending upon how large each piece is and how tightly they are packed. Since there will always be airspace between the chunks you're probably only getting about 85 cubic feet of actual wood in that 128 cubic foot "box."

Economics of Wood Heat

We are often asked how much it costs to heat with wood. That's a complicated answer. In our case we heat with wood because it's the cheapest resource we have available. We seldom buy wood and my labor incurs no out-of-pocket expense so the only cash outlay we have is for equipment, fuel and insurance for the truck. Chainsaws last for many years as does our work truck which is only used periodically during the year. I use less than five gallons of gasoline per year for the chainsaws and spend about $100 per year on chains. I use anywhere from ten to thirty gallons of gasoline per year in the truck depending upon where I procure my wood. That's not much money considering our cold climate which requires heat at least part of the day for nine-months of the year.

If you're starting from scratch and need to purchase a saw, truck and whatever else you need it can get pretty pricey! However, saws last for years as do wood hauling trucks or trailers so those expenses average out over the years. Most people could purchase a cheap trailer to pull behind their SUV and a small, homeowners saw and be in business for less than $500 with some judicious shopping.

Wood can often be acquired for free. Go for a drive after a windstorm and offer to cut up and haul off the limbs that have fallen. Find someone who wants some trees taken out. (Be careful here! I don't advise newcomers to cut down trees near homes, buildings or power lines. Get some experience first.)

I was cutting a tree out on my mother's property and had one of her neighbors ask me to cut down one on his place across the street. The word will get around. Post notices on public bulletin boards and use free internet resources to advertise. Word will get around and you'll find yourself with more work than you can handle if you do a good job and clean up your mess afterward.

If you're purchasing wood it's not difficult to estimate how much it will cost per year. If you've always used a different type of energy to heat your home you can use the comparisons below and the spreadsheet provided to get an idea of how much wood you'd need to get through a winter. Then you can decide if it's cheaper to heat with wood.

To get an idea of how wood compares to other fuels use the information below and the spreadsheet provided.

One cubic foot of natural gas = 1,000 BTU's

89

One gallon of #2 fuel oil =132,000 BTU's
One gallon of HD5 propane = 91,700 BTU's
One ton of coal = 16 million BTU's
One kW of electricity = 3,413 BTU's
One ton of wood pellets = 13.9 million BTU's
One cord of white birch = 20.3 million BTU's

For example one cord of white birch produces approximately 20,300,000 BTU's of energy. Divide that by 132,000 BTU's (energy rating of one gallon of fuel oil) and you will need almost 154 gallons of fuel oil to equal the heat output of one cord of white birch.

Remember, this is a guideline for comparison purposes only. Actual energy output will most likely vary depending on the situation. The amount of energy contained in wood depends on it's resin and moisture content and it's density. A general rule is that all wood dried to the same moisture content contains about the same heat value per pound. But by volume (the way wood is usually sold) it's a different story.

Using our example of Larch vs. Pine in the second paragraph we can go to the spreadsheet and see that the heat value of one cord (128 cubic feet by volume) of Larch is 20.8 million BTU's. The same volume (one cord) of Yellow Pine has a heat value of 15.8 million BTU's. That's approximately twenty-five percent less heat per cord when compared to Larch. Divide the purchase price by the heat volume and you'll see that the cost of burning Larch is approximately $4.81 per million BTU's while the cost of burning Yellow pine is $5.69 per million BTU's. The best deal is the Larch at $100.00 per cord.

Firewood Ratings	Heat Value	Million BTU's per Cord	Easy to Split?	Overall Rating

Alder	Medium	14.8	Yes	Poor
Apple	High	26.5	No	Medium
Ash, Black	Medium	19.1	Yes	Excellent
Ash, White, Green	High	23.6	Yes	Excellent
Aspen	Low	14.7	Yes	Fair
Basswood	Low	13.5	Yes	Fair
Beech	High	25	Yes	Excellent
Birch, Black	High	26.8	Yes	Excellent
Birch, White, Gray, Paper	Medium	20.3	Yes	Excellent
Birch, Yellow	High	23.6	Yes	Excellent
Boxelder	Low	17.9	No	Fair
Butternut	Low	14.5	Yes	Poor
Catalpa	Low	16.4	No	Poor
Cedar, White, Red	Medium	17.5	Yes	Good
Cherry	Medium	20	Yes	Good
Chestnut	Low	12.9	Yes	Poor
Cottonwood	Low	13.5	Yes	Fair
Cypress	Medium		Yes	Fair
Dogwood	High	30.4	Yes	Excellent
Douglas Fir	High	21.4	Yes	Good
Eastern	High	27.3	No	Excellent

91

Hornbeam				
Elm, White, American	Medium	19.5	No	Fair
Eucalyptus	High	33.5	No	Fair
Fir, Balsam	Low	14.3	Yes	Poor
Gum	Medium	18.5	No	Fair
Hackberry	Medium	20.8	Yes	Excellent
Hawthorn	High		Medium	Good
Hemlock	Low	15.9		Fair
Hickory	High	27.7	Medium	Excellent
Locust, Black	High	26.8	No	Excellent
Locust, Honey	High	25.8	Medium	Excellent
Maple, Hard	High	29.7	Yes	Excellent
Maple, Soft, Red	Medium	18.7	Yes	Excellent
Maple, Sugar	High	24	No	Good
Oak, Red	High	21.7	No	Excellent
Oak, White	High	25.7	No	Excellent
Pecan	High		Yes	Excellent
Pine, Norway, Jack, Pinch	Low	17.1	Yes	Fair
Pine, Ponderosa	Low	15.2	Yes	Fair

Pine, Sugar	Low	15.8	Yes	Fair
Pine, White	Low	14.3	Yes	Fair
Pine, Yellow	Low	15.8	Yes	Good
Poplar, Yellow	Low	16	Yes	Poor
Redwood	Medium	18.8	Yes	Fair
Spruce	Low	14.5	Yes	Poor
Sycamore	Medium	18.5	No	Fair
Tamarack/Larch	Medium	20.8	Yes	Fair
Walnut	Medium	20	Yes	Good
Willow	Low	14.5	Yes	Poor

This firewood size chunk of pine weighs twenty-three pounds.
Almost Fourteen pounds of that is water weight.
That's the equivalent of the two jugs of water standing beside it.

Seasoning

Seasoning is just another term for drying wood. When a live tree is cut down, sixty percent or more of it's weight may be water. This is called "green" wood and the moisture in it causes problems when you burn it. A large percentage of the heat must be used to evaporate all of that water before the wood fibers can burn. As this water evaporates it's trying to put out your fire just as if you were sprinkling water on it. You end up with a cold fire. A cold fire not only gives off less heat, it also produces creosote which clogs chimneys and is the number one cause of chimney fires. Wood is considered properly seasoned when the moisture content is reduced below twenty-percent.

When a tree dries, very little moisture escapes through the sides, traveling instead through the cut ends. The best way to dry firewood is to cut it into stove length and stack it where air can circulate through it. The shorter the wood and the better the air circulation the faster it will dry. It's seldom necessary to season stove length wood longer than six months. However, longer wood may need a year or more to season properly. Unless you live in a climate where rain and high humidity are the norm, covering wood doesn't speed things up much. Likewise, splitting the wood helps a little but again, the improvement is minimal.

Splitting

There are some good reasons to split firewood. First, large diameter logs that won't fit through the door of your stove must be split. Similarly, if the pieces are too heavy it's best to split them. Finally, split wood is easier to ignite. When you split wood you leave at least one edge sharp. Because the mass at the edge is smaller it heats faster and reaches the ignition point sooner than wood that's in the "round." Split wood often has splinters protruding from the wood. These splinters also ignite easily and provide more heat to get the log burning quicker.

Splitting problem wood is simple if you have a motorized splitter. However, if you're doing it by hand you'll want to target wood that's easier to split. The spreadsheet included has a column rating the different types of wood by how easy or difficult they are to split. Again, use this as a general guide. I know from personal experience that some trees that should be easy to split aren't due to anomalies like twisted grain or multiple or large knots. It's also easier to split dry wood than green wood. Wood with a high moisture content tends to be spongy and grips the maul or wedge instead of splitting.

Purchasing Firewood

If you buy firewood be sure that you and the seller are talking about the same amount of wood. We've already discussed the measurements of a "full cord" of wood (four feet wide, four feet high and eight feet long). Sometimes merchants sell what's called a "face" cord (AKA, "rank," "rick," "stove cord," or "fireplace cord"). A "Face cord" is a stack of wood that is four feet high and eight feet long but is only as deep as the pieces of firewood. For example, when the wood is sold in "stove length" (which is usually 16 inches long) a face cord will measure four feet by eight feet by 16 inches deep which is one-third of a full cord of wood.

Be sure that the wood is seasoned and, if cut to length, know what that length is. It will do you little good if you purchase a cord of wood cut to 20 inch lengths when your stove will only hold pieces sixteen inches long! Also find out if it's split and if so, how small. I've seen split firewood so large it still wouldn't fit the firebox of our stove. Save yourself a headache and find out before you order it.

Firewood, is a commonly available renewable energy source that's relatively clean, efficient, and safe. It's a way to utilize downed trees that would otherwise be disposed of in a landfill. Whether you buy your firewood or cut it yourself it pays to know which woods will work the best for you.

Chapter Six – Firewood Splitting

Our wood stove is our only heat source so filling the woodshed is serious business. We usually go through six to eight cords of firewood per year and almost every piece has to be split. We split firewood for three reasons. First, to make it small enough to fit in our stove. Second, to make large pieces easier to handle. Third, split wood is easier to ignite.

Choosing an Ax or Maul

Some people use the term splitting ax and splitting maul to describe the same tools. However there is difference. A splitting ax usually weighs between three and four pounds whereas a splitting maul will tip the scales at anywhere from six to twelve pounds.

It's important to understand the difference between splitting and cutting wood. Cutting is performed across the grain while splitting goes with the grain. Felling axes, designed to cut through the wood fibers, have a thin blade that bites deep into the grain. Splitting axes have a thick blade that wedges wood fibers apart. Most axes sold today are a compromise between the two which means they don't work really well for either task.

Photo One

In photo #1 you'll see three different types of splitting mauls and a splitting wedge. On the left is a maul I purchased at a large discount store years ago. It has a tubular steel handle with a wide, heavy, triangular shaped head. It tips the scales at twelve pounds. The maul in the center with an ax type head weighs about six pounds. The head is narrow and sharp and the sides have a slight hollow grind. The maul at the right is a compromise between the first two. It weighs eight pounds and has a head width close to the second maul but it has a convex profile in the front half. All of these designs will split wood but the real question is which is best?

98

It would seem to make sense that heavier is better but that's not always the case. For most men I'd recommend mauls in the eight to ten pound range. For women and young teens it might be better to get a six pound maul or a good splitting ax in the three to four pound range. Control is far more important than inertia. With a lighter maul or ax you can always apply some extra muscle in the down stroke to make it split better. If it's too heavy you'll wear yourself out quicker and possibly lose control of the maul when swinging it.

I'm a big fan of plastic/fiberglass handles. Sooner or later you're going to overshoot your mark and bring the handle down over the edge of the wood. A wood handle almost always breaks when that happens. Fiberglass handles will usually survive. The new fiberglass handles with a rubber sleeve in the eye of the head are even better. The thick rubber absorbs a lot of the inertia, saving the handle. Steel handles are a pain, literally. Even with foam rubber sleeves they transfer a lot of vibration to your hands. In addition steel handles are cold in winter compared to wood or fiberglass handles.

There are two different handle designs where they attach to the head of the maul. The two mauls with fiberglass handles in photo #1 are a sledge hammer type handle. If you look at the top of the maul they are shaped like an oval. The other type is more of a tear drop shape like a single bit ax. In my experience both designs are good.

The part of the handle you grip with your hands should be oval ... *not round*! The oval shape gives your hands reference points that make it easier to grip and hold the maul's head in a vertical position when you swing it. A round handle feels the same all the way around and your hands have no reference points. Every time you pick it up you have to check the alignment of your hands with the mauls head. If it's a little crooked coming down the maul may glance off when it hits the wood. The maul at the left in Photo

One has a round handle. I gave it away a couple of years ago.

Be sure the head is secured to the handle. Wood handles are prone to loosen over time. The bond on fiberglass handles can also come loose so always check the head before using the maul. If the head comes off the handle it will probably destroy whatever is in it's path.

Photo 2

Before purchasing a maul or ax check to see that the head is on straight. (See photo 2) The blade's edge should be in line with the center of the handle when you sight down it's length. You might have to look over several at the store until you find one that's right. If you replace the handle be sure it's properly aligned with the head.

Photo 3

So, does head shape matter? In some cases, yes. What I've found is that the "ax type" taper found on the maul in photo 3 works better in wood with knots in it. When you hit a knot you've transitioned from traveling with the grain to cutting through it. The maul in photo 2 will split the wood apart until it hit's a knot then it will "bash" it's way through. If the knot is small it doesn't matter. However if it's an inch or more in diameter it can be a problem.

Our favorite mauls have a rounded profile at the cutting edge. In photo 1, the maul at the left has a straight edge like the wedge at the front of the photo. The cutting edges on the mauls in the center and right have a rounded contour much like an ax. In my experience these work a little better than a straight edge.

Most manufacturer's do not recommend that you use the "hammer end" (the poll) of the maul for pounding. If you use it for pounding the head will eventually "broom" but then so will a sledge hammer. Overall it's probably best to follow the manufacturer's recommendation.

Never use an ax or maul like a wedge. If you pound on the back of the head to drive it through the wood you'll swell the poll and spread the eye. After that you'll never get a handle to fit right.

Wedges

Splitting wedges come in various shapes and sizes. I've used most of them at one time or another and always come back to the old classic shown in photo #1. You'll see advertisements showing blocks of firewood "exploding" into multiple pieces by fancy wedges and that happens occasionally (but most of the time it doesn't work that way in real life). The main reason I always come back to "old reliable" is that they'll cut through knots where the pointy wedges will either stick in them or slither around them.

Whatever kind you purchase it's best to have at least two. Some wood is "stringy" and you can drive a wedge all the way through it and not split it completely. Your first wedge will be stuck tight and you'll need another wedge or chainsaw to finish the job.

Do not confuse felling wedges with splitting wedges. A felling wedge is used when you're cutting down a tree to keep the kerf open and to help the tree fall the right direction. They're made out of plastic or wood so that if you jam it against the saw's chain it won't damage the chain. They're also half the thickness of a splitting wedge. Splitting wedges are bigger and heavier and made of steel.

Splitting or "Chopping" Blocks

I use a splitting block for three reasons. First, it gets the wood up higher so that the maul hits squarely on the wood being split. Second, the block provides a hard surface under the piece I'm splitting. If you just set the piece to be split on the ground the soil will provide a cushioning effect, much like the shock absorber on your car. Splitting blocks minimize this so that the maximum force is transmitted by the maul to the wood. The final reason is that splitting blocks protect the maul from rocks or gravel those times it's driven through the piece being split.

I use the largest section of firewood for my splitting block but that may not work for everyone. You may need one that's higher or lower depending upon your height, arm or leg length, and the length of the pieces being split. I like the maul's handle to be parallel with the ground when the head comes into contact with the top of the wood being split. You may have to experiment to find what's right for you.

Tips for Difficult Wood

Knots, twisted grain, and green wood!
A knot is a tree branch that the trunk has grown around. The reason they make splitting difficult is because the grain in the knot is ninety-degrees to the grain in the trunk. It's like nature's version of re-bar. A splitting maul doesn't "cut" wood. It rips it apart following the grain of the wood. Knots interrupt this splitting action. It's best to split wood so that the split is between the knots rather than through them. Pieces with a lot of large knots are best split with a motorized splitter or a saw.

Twisted grain is another problem child of the splitting world (see photo four). In these instances, instead of the grain running straight up the trunk it grows in a spiral pattern like a barber pole. I use a wedge driven through the center of the wood. There's not much twist to the grain through the center. If you use a wedge or maul on the outer edges of the wood you'll have to drive them through at the same angle as the twist. If you try to drive the wedge straight down it will be cutting through the wood fibers instead of splitting them apart.

Green wood is a problem because it's spongy. Wedges and mauls just stick in the wood instead of splitting it. If the wood is green the best thing to do is cut it to firewood lengths and set it aside to season (one to four months). I believe this is where the idea originated that wood splits easier when it's cold. The concept is that the moisture in the wood freezes so the wood is more brittle and splits easier.

What has usually happened is that the wood has been drying out during the transition between summer and winter and it splits easier because it's seasoned rather than frozen. Even if you do get it split, frozen green wood is still green wood. When you try to burn it, it's going to be difficult to ignite and will put out less heat because the fire will have to evaporate the water left in the wood before it can burn the wood itself. Burning green wood is like throwing wet newspapers on the fire.

The final challenge to splitting wood is when you split large rounds. When you cut down a large tree (anything with a trunk diameter above eighteen inches) the sheer mass can make even easy splitting wood difficult. It's like the difference between ripping a small-town newspaper apart verses ripping the Los Angeles phone book apart.

I use a couple of different techniques on large rounds. The first is to use wedges and split them through the center. This works best if you can follow an existing crack in the wood (see photo 4).

Photo Four

The second method is to begin by splitting at the outside edge and work your way around, gradually reducing the size on the round (see photo 5).

Photo Five

Power Splitters

If you have a stack of difficult wood you may want to rent a motorized splitter. There are two types available: vertical and horizontal. With horizontal splitters you'll have to lift each piece of wood up and hold it on the bed while you split it. With a vertical splitter you can roll the pieces over to it and set them on a plate under the splitter. The best are those that can be used both ways. Either type will make splitting problem wood much easier.

I wouldn't bother with cheap "hand pump" units or gizmos that have the splitting wedge mounted to a slide. They'll do the job but they are slow and labor intensive. The advantage is that you can put the cutting edge on the exact place you want to hit (in case you aren't too good at swinging a maul or sledge accurately.)

How small you split your firewood is a personal choice. I usually split ours small enough that I can pick it up with one hand. The reason being that even though larger pieces will fit in our stove the smaller chunks are easier to handle, especially for my wife and children.

Be Safe

Clear out a safe place to split your wood. Take the ax or maul by the head and hold it horizontally at arm's length and slowly pivot in a full circle. This is your safe zone. Remove anything that might interfere with your swing. Keep everyone out while you're working.

Minimize distractions. There should be no blaring radios, children playing nearby, or pets wandering through. Wear good boots, (preferably with steel toes) and gloves that provide a good grip.

Check handles for splits and heads for looseness. Never swing a maul or ax in a direction that someone could be injured if the head comes off.

Check wedges for broomed ends. This occurs after repeated

pounding when driving the wedge through wood. Eventually the end flares outward leaving jagged shards around the outer edge. These can break off under impact and fly like a bullet, hitting with enough force to penetrate skin and eyes. Periodically inspect your wedges and grind them back to factory profiles.

Don't split wood when you are fatigued. Tired muscles don't react like they should and if you miss your mark the maul can easily break a leg, foot, our any other part of your body that tries to stop it's momentum. You may have to limit splitting time until you develop the muscles and stamina needed to maintain control for longer sessions.

Over the years I've had a lot of people try to talk me into purchasing a motorized wood splitter. I've continually resisted. If you want one more power to you. I think they're loud, smelly, expensive and unnecessary. (And it's just one more thing to break and need repairs.)

It might be a guy thing but there's something satisfying about a well aimed swing, driving a splitting maul through a chunk of firewood. And I like the way my shoulders and arms have that tired but good feeling after a few hours of splitting wood.

The final perk of harvesting our own firewood is spending those cold, winter days basking in the warmth of a wood burning stove in our off-grid cabin while reading a book.

Conclusion

Chainsaws are not forgiving so be safety conscious at all times. Trees are not forgiving either. We live in logging country and it's one of the most dangerous professions on earth. We personally know several people who have survived some pretty catastrophic accidents in the woods. Some will never fully recover from the injuries they sustained.

I'm not writing this to scare you away but to instill some caution. The main purpose in writing this book was to help you avoid the pitfalls many new woodcutters fall into. In many ways woodcutting is like driving a vehicle: one moment of carelessness can usher in a lifetime of pain, suffering or death so keep your head about you at all times!

But now it's time to get out and put into practice what you've learned. Just remember to start small in both equipment and trees. Move to larger and more challenging projects as your skill increases. Most importantly though, be safe and enjoy your time in the woods.

The End

If you enjoyed this book you'll want to check out some of the other books written by this author. Go to the Web Page for Amazon Books and type in a search for the author's name. You'll bring up titles like:

Creating the Low-Budget Homestead

The Gun Guide for People Who Know Nothing About Firearms

The Beginner's Guide to Reloading Ammunition: With Space and Money Saving Tips for Apartment Dwellers and Those on a Budget

You can find my blog by going to: http://livinglifeoff-grid.blogspot.com/. This chronicles our life as off-grid, (almost) self-sufficient homesteaders on our 20 acre homestead in northwestern, Montana.

My wife also has numerous books published. Type in a search on the Amazon Books site for Susan Gregersen.

She's a prolific writer and some of her best seller's include (but are not limited to):

Poverty Prepping: How to Stock Up for Tomorrow When You Can't Afford to Eat Today

Food Storage: Preserving Fruits, Nuts and Seeds

Food Storage: Preserving Meat, Dairy and Eggs

And many more listings in both fiction and non-fiction books.

Her blog can be viewed at: http://povertyprepping.blogspot.com/

Printed in Great Britain
by Amazon.co.uk, Ltd.,
Marston Gate.